O is for old school

WIDE EYED EDITIONS

This is a hip-hop alphabet for B. I. G. people who used to be dope.

My friends Robbie and Rachel were so dope, but then they had a baby boy. So I wrote this book to let him know that his parents weren't always as wack as they are right now.

Inside you'll learn that when a baby comes along, the words and phrases of hip-hop take on new meanings; now Peace comes at naptime, a Hood is worn on a head, and when they Flow it's going to get wet.

This book is your chance to remember your old school days while your kid learns their ABC's like a G.

Word to the muthas . . . and the poppas.

A

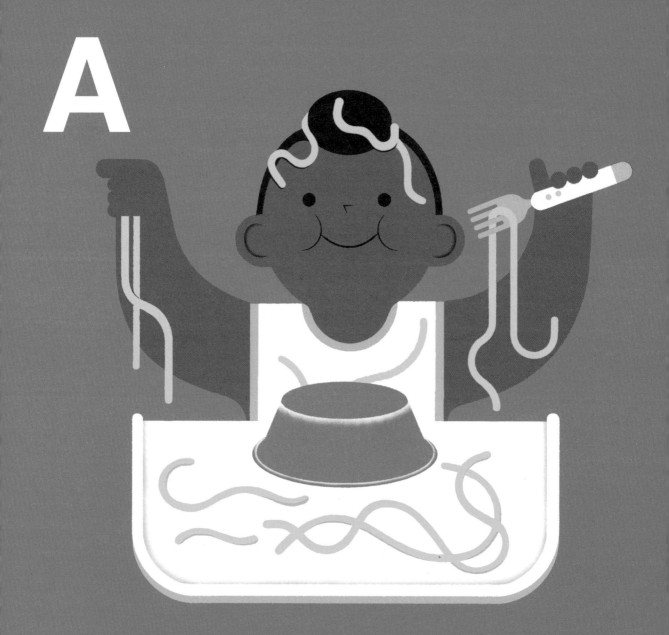

is for **All good**

B

is for **Ballin'**

C

is for **Crib**

D

is for **Dawg**

E

is for **Eazy**

F

is for **Flow**

G

is for **Grill**

H

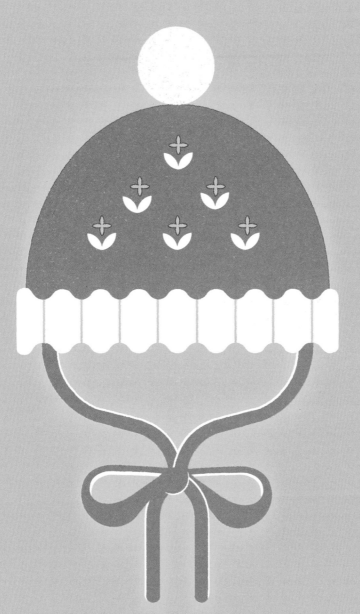

is for **Hood**

I is for **Ice**

J

is for **Juice**

K

is for **Kick it!**

L

is for **Lil'**

M

is for **Mutha**

N

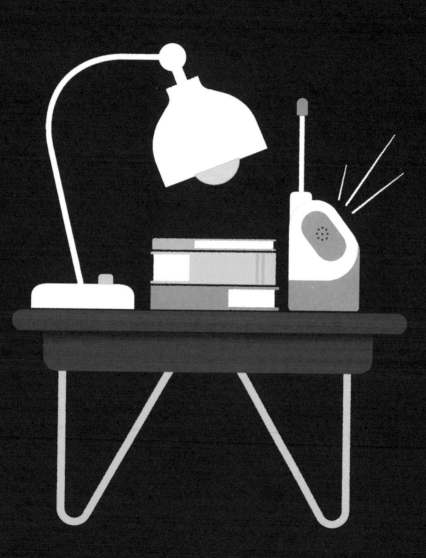

is for **Non-stop**

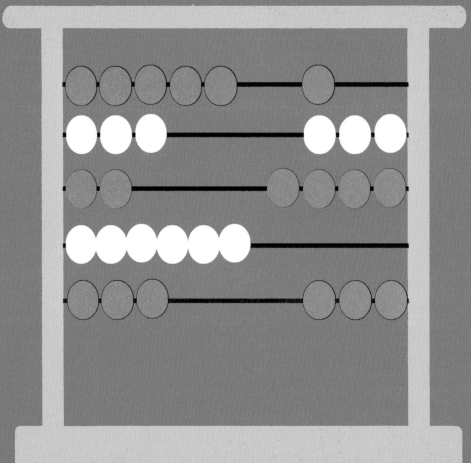

is for **Old school**

P

is for **Peace**

Q

is for **Quit playin'**

R

is for **Rollin'**

S

is for **Sucka**

T

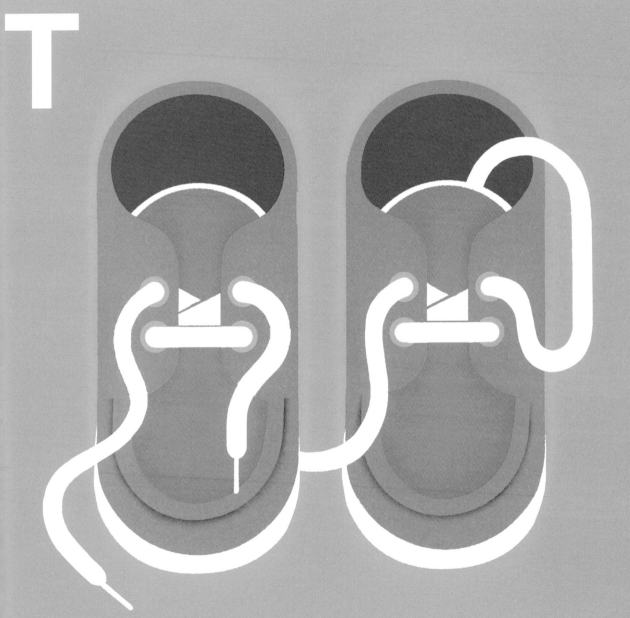

is for **Trippin'**

U

is for **U da bomb!**

V

is for **Vibin'**

W

is for **Wack**

X

is for **Xplicit content**

Y

is for Yo yo!

Z

is for **Zero chill**

word up

ALL GOOD

Adjective	Everything's fine.
An exclamation	Don't worry.

BALLIN'

Verb	Living successfully.
Verb	Playing basketball.

CRIB

Noun	One's place of residence; located in one's hood (see H).

DAWG

Noun	One's close friend.

EAZY

Adjective	To act casually.
A greeting	Hello.

FLOW

Noun	The style in which someone rhymes, intonates, and enunciates.

GRILL

Noun	A metal plate moulded to one's teeth often inlaid with precious stones.
Noun	One's personal business.

HOOD

Noun	An area in which one lives, or has lived in. Short for neighborhood. The location of one's crib (see C).

ICE

Noun	Expensive diamond jewelry.

JUICE

Adjective	Respect and credibility.
An exclamation	Overwhelmingly good.

KICK IT!

Verb	To spend quality time with someone while not doing anything in particular.

LIL'

Adjective	Meaning little.
Prefix	Placed before one's name to imply impishness.

MUTHA

Noun	One's mother.
An exclamation	Used to exaggerate an amount.

NON-STOP

Adverb	Used to describe a situation, activity, or party that won't end for a long time.

OLD SCHOOL

Adjective	From an early era, to be viewed with respect.

PEACE

A greeting	Hello.
A greeting	Goodbye.

QUIT PLAYIN'

Interjection	Stop acting like a fool.

ROLLIN'

Verb	Hanging out with friends.
Verb	Driving an automobile.

SUCKA

Noun	Someone uncool, no good, or talentless.

TRIPPIN'

Verb	To get excited about something.
Verb	To get upset over nothing.

U DA BOMB!

An expression	You are really wonderful.

VIBIN'

Verb	Getting along well with someone.
Verb	Feeling relaxed.
Verb	Listening to pleasing music.

WACK

Adjective	Someone or something uncool, no good, or talentless.

XPLICIT CONTENT

Adjective	Lyrics deemed inappropriate for a younger audience.

YO YO!

A greeting	Hello.

ZERO CHILL

Adjective	Acting in an irrational or reckless manner.

Brimming with creative inspiration, how-to projects, and useful information to enrich your everyday life, Quarto Knows is a favourite destination for those pursuing their interests and passions. Visit our site and dig deeper with our books into your area of interest: Quarto Creates, Quarto Cooks, Quarto Homes, Quarto Lives, Quarto Drives, Quarto Explores, Quarto Gifts, or Quarto Kids.

Inspiring | Educating | Creating | Entertaining

A catalogue record for this book is available from the British Library.

ISBN 978-1-78603-137-2

The illustrations were created digitally
Set in Helvetica

Published by Jenny Broom and Rachel Williams
Designed by Nicola Price
Edited by Katie Cotton
Production by Jenny Cundill and Kate O'Riordan

Manufactured in Guangdong, China. CC082019

9 8 7 6 5